THIS BOOK BELONGS TO

_____

THANK YOU TO ALL THE HARD WORKING, CREATIVE, AND INSPIRATIONAL MINDS THAT WERE INVOLVED IN THE CREATION OF THIS REVOLUTIONARY AND EXPERIENTIAL BOOK. THIS BOOK IS DEDICATED TO ALL THE READERS WHO HAVE THE IMAGINATION AND PASSION FOR LEARNING AND ADVENTURE.

TRULY,

Scott Jochim

PRESIDENT

Read it. See it. Be it.

DIGITAL TECH FRONTIER, LLC. ARIZONA
WWW.POPARBOOKS.COM

ISBN 978-0-9830127-2-6

COPYRIGHT © 2011 DIGITAL TECH FRONTIER, LLC.
TEXT AND DESIGN BY ROBERT SIDDELL
PRODUCTION AND DESIGN BY SCOTT JOCHIM
3D ART AND ANIMATIONS BY SHROX
GRAPHIC DESIGN BY LYNN CUPAN
COVER & GRAPHIC DESIGN BY VERONICA MARTINEZ

PRINTED IN CHINA

CONSTRUCTION ZONE...

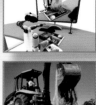

Tools Needed For Construction Site!

1

Go to www.PoparToys.com/software

2

Find the software that matches this book

3

Download and install the software

Remove the "i" paddle to use throughout the entire book

What are the minimum computer system requirements to view Augmented Reality in Popar™ Books?

PC Hardware:
- A webcam
- CPU-Pentium 3 800MHz or higher processor. 1200MHz recommended
- RAM-500 MB or above recommended
- Graphics card-3D accelerated graphics card

PC Operating System:
- Windows XP SP2 or above, Windows Vista, Windows 7

Droid:
- Droid 4.0 or Higher

Macintosh Hardware:
- A webcam
- CPU-Intel Core 2 Duo 2.0 GHz or above
- RAM-500 MB or above recommended
- Graphics card-3D accelerated graphics card

Mactintosh Operating System:
- Mac OS 10.4, 10.5 and 10.6

IOS:
- iPhone 4/4s, iPad 2/3 or Higher

ANDROID APP ON
► Google play

Available on the
App Store

HERE'S HOW IT WORKS...

What are Popar™ Books?

Popar™ Books use Augmented Reality (AR) technology to create an immersive reading experience that will allow the user to see their books come alive with incredible virtually "real" 3D objects and animations that will pop off the page. Popar™ Books are designed to change the way we interact and experience stories, adventures, and learning.

What is Augmented Reality (AR)?

Our Augmented Reality (AR) is a ground-breaking concept that uses a computer, a webcam, and special black and white patterned markers to make amazing 3D objects and animations appear in the real world that provide a high degree of engaging interaction that maintain interest in all of the Popar™ Book series.

What do I need to see Augmented Reality in my Popar™ Book?

- Computer or mobile device that meets the minimum system requirements
- A webcam or mobile device
- Popar™ Books software
- Popar™ Books

1

First you will need to hook up your webcam to your computers USB.
*Note: For mobile users see step 2.

2

Then download the Popar™ Books installation software from www.PoparToys.com/software.
*Note: Mobile users download the Popar™ Construction 3D Book app.

3 Run the Popar™ Books software

4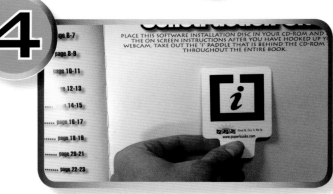

Go to page three and take out the "i" paddle.
*Note: "i" paddle will not be needed with mobile devices.

5

Next position your webcam or mobile device, so that it has a view of the entire right page of the Popar™ Book when the book is open.

READ-ALONG INSTRUCTIONS

*Note: Mobile users see in app tutorial for read along instructions

A

On the bottom of every single right hand page is a black & white Augmented Reality (AR) marker that will display a 3D animation when in view of the webcam.

B

In order to play the interactive virtual reality game on every page, the black & white Augmented Reality marker and the "i" paddle must both be in view of the webcam. Simply bring the "i" paddle close to the Augmented Reality marker or close to the center of the page to play the game.

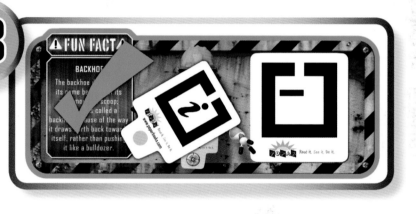

C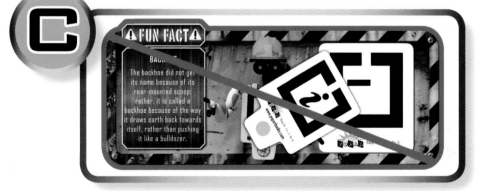

Do not overlap the black and white Augmented Reality markers or the animation and model will not appear.

D

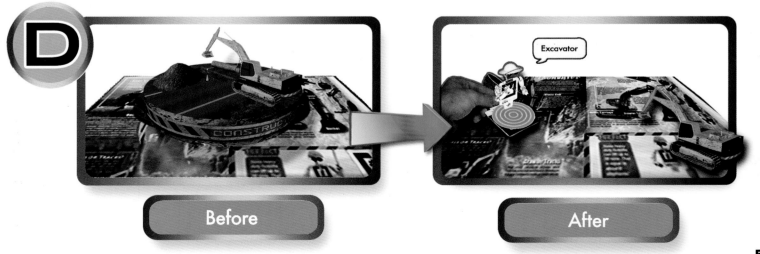

Before

After

DIPPER

THIS IS THE PIECE WHICH CARRIES THE BUCKET AND IS ALSO KNOWN AS THE DIPPERSTICK.

REAR BUCKET

THE REAR BUCKET HAS NARROW TEETH THAT ARE GREAT FOR DIGGING.

CAB

THE SWIVEL SEAT ALLOWS THE DRIVER TO FACE EITHER BUCKET. THERE ARE CONTROLS IN THE CAB THAT ALLOW THE OPERATOR TO MOVE EITHER BUCKET UP OR DOWN.

BOOM

THE SECTION OF THE ARM CLOSEST TO THE VEHICLE IS KNOWN AS THE BOOM. THE BOOM IS ATTACHED TO THE VEHICLE THROUGH A PIVOT WHICH ALLOWS THE ARM TO TURN LEFT AND RIGHT 200°.

STABILIZER LEGS

THESE LEGS HELP SECURE THE BACKHOE TO THE GROUND SO THAT THE MACHINE IS COMPLETELY STABILIZED WHEN IT IS DIGGING AND LOADING MATERIALS.

WHEELS

THE BIG WHEELS WITH DEEP TREAD HELP THE BACKHOE KEEP ITS TRACKING IN MUD OR ROUGH TERRAIN.

DIG, SCOOP AND SO MUCH MORE

A BACKHOE CAN DIG A LOT OF DIRT. BUT DID YOU KNOW A BACKHOE CAN ALSO CRUSH PAVEMENT, LIFT HEAVY CONCRETE BLOCKS, AND DRILL DEEP HOLES INTO THE HARDEST GROUND?

BACKHOE

WHEN IT'S TIME TO DIG A HOLE THAT DOES NOT REQUIRE AN EXCAVATOR, THE BACKHOE IS THE PERFECT VEHICLE TO USE. A BACKHOE IS A PIECE OF EXCAVATING EQUIPMENT OR DIGGER THAT HAS A DIGGING BUCKET ON THE ONE END AND A LOADING BUCKET ON THE OTHER END.

FRONT BUCKET

THIS BUCKET IS VERY WIDE SO THAT IT CAN LIFT AND LOAD A LOT OF MATERIAL INTO THE BACK OF A DUMP TRUCK OR JUST MOVE MATERIALS OUT OF THE WAY.

⚠ FUN FACT ⚠

BACKHOE

The backhoe did not get its name because of its rear-mounted scoop; rather, it is called a backhoe because of the way it draws earth back towards itself, rather than pushing it like a bulldozer.

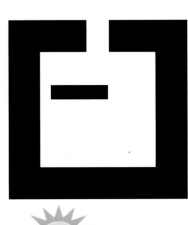

POPAR Read It. See It. Be It.

DUMP TRUCKS WORK TOGETHER WITH OTHER MACHINES SUCH AS EXCAVATORS AND BACKHOES TO CLEAR DIRT, ROCKS, AND OTHER MATERIALS OUT OF THE JOB SITE.

HEAVY HAULERS

HAUL TRUCK CAPACITIES RANGE FROM 50 SHORT TONS TO 400 SHORT TONS.

HAUL TRUCKS ARE OFF-HIGHWAY, TWO-AXLE, RIGID DUMP TRUCKS SPECIFICALLY ENGINEERED FOR USE IN HIGH PRODUCTION MINING AND HEAVY-DUTY CONSTRUCTION ENVIRONMENTS.

THESE TRUCKS ARE SO HUGE THAT A HUMAN CAN FIT INTO THE WHEEL.

AFTER ALL THE OTHER BIG MACHINES DIG HOLES AND PUSH THE MATERIALS SOMEWHERE, WE NEED TO GET THE DIRT AND OTHER MATERIALS OUT OF THE WAY FOR THE OTHER PIECES OF EQUIPMENT TO COME IN.

DUMP TRUCK

At some construction sites, dump trucks are used to bring in materials such as rocks and dirt to help with the building.

Hinge

A typical dump truck is equipped with a hydraulically operated hinge at the rear which allows for the front to be lifted up to dump the contents on the ground behind the truck.

⚠ FUN FACT ⚠

DUMP TRUCK

Some super dump trucks can carry over 100 tons of material at one time. That's the same as carrying over 100 hippos.

BULLDOZER

BULLDOZERS ARE GREAT AT CLEARING THE GROUND BEFORE CONSTRUCTION STARTS.

THE BULLDOZER IS A CRAWLER EQUIPPED WITH A METAL PLATE THAT IS USED TO PUSH LARGE QUANTITIES OF SOIL, SAND, STONES, AND RUBBLE DURING CONSTRUCTION WORK. IT IS ALSO TYPICALLY EQUIPPED AT THE OTHER END WITH A CLAW-LIKE DEVICE TO LOOSEN COMPACTED MATERIALS.

AFTER THE EXCAVATOR DIGS A HOLE, WE NEED TO GET THAT DIRT OUT OF THE WAY.

Blade

THE BULLDOZER BLADE IS A HEAVY METAL PLATE ON THE FRONT OF THE TRACTOR THAT IS USED TO PUSH OBJECTS SUCH AS SAND, SOIL, AND DEBRIS. DOZER BLADES USUALLY COME IN THREE VARIETIES: S-BLADE, U-BLADE, AND AN SU COMBINATION BLADE.

Roof

SOME BULLDOZERS HAVE WINDOWS IN THEIR CAB AND OTHERS DO NOT DEPENDING ON HOW DIRTY THE JOB SITE IS. THE ROOF OF THE CAB IS CALLED THE CANOPY, AND IS ALSO THERE FOR PROTECTION FROM FALLING DEBRIS.

Crawler Tracks

THE LARGE STEEL BELTS AT THE BOTTOM OF THE BULLDOZER ARE THE CRAWLER TRACKS THAT HELP IT MOVE FORWARDS AND BACKWARDS VERY EASILY ON LOOSE GROUND.

Ripper

THE RIPPER IS THE LONG CLAW-LIKE DEVICE ON THE BACK OF THE BULLDOZER. THE RIPPER BREAKS THE GROUND SURFACE ROCK INTO SMALL RUBBLE THAT IS EASY TO HANDLE AND TRANSPORT. ALSO, HARD EARTH CAN BE RIPPED AND DE-COMPACTED TO ALLOW PLANTING OF ORCHARDS WHERE TREES COULD NOT OTHERWISE GROW.

BULLDOZERS AT WORK!

CLEARING A WOODED AREA   CLEARING BIG BOULDERS   6-WAY BLADE ATTACHMENT   U-BLADE ATTACHMENT

11

⚠ FUN FACT ⚠

BULLDOZER

Bulldozers only go 6 miles per hour. This is one big machine that will lose in a race.

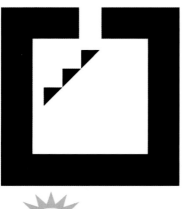

THE OVERHEAD GUARD IS A METAL ROOF SUPPORTED BY POSTS AT EACH CORNER OF THE CAB THAT HELPS TO PROTECT THE OPERATOR FROM ANY FALLING OBJECTS.

INTERNAL COMBUSTION (IC) FORKLIFTS ARE IDEAL FOR OUTDOOR USE, BUT IF FUELED BY PROPANE, THEY CAN BE USED INDOORS OR OUTDOORS.

Mast

THE MAST IS THE ASSEMBLY THAT DOES THE WORK OF RAISING AND LOWERING THE LOAD.

Carriage

THE CARRIAGE IS THE COMPONENT FOR MOUNTING FORKS AND OTHER ATTACHMENTS.

ELECTRIC FORKLIFTS ARE IDEAL FOR WORKING INDOORS IN MANY TYPES OF BUSINESSES. ELECTRIC FORKLIFTS CAN BE OPERATED OUTDOORS, TYPICALLY ONLY ON DRY, WELL-PAVED SURFACES.

FORKLIFT

WHENEVER YOU NEED TO MOVE, LIFT, AND TRANSPORT MATERIALS SUCH AS A PALLET OF WOOD, CEMENT BLOCKS, OR BUILDING MATERIALS, A FORKLIFT IS THE PERFECT MACHINE FOR YOU TO USE.

Cab

THE CAB IS THE AREA THAT CONTAINS A SEAT FOR THE OPERATOR ALONG WITH THE CONTROL PEDALS, A STEERING WHEEL, LEVERS, AND SWITCHES. THE CAB AREA MAY BE OPEN AIR OR ENCLOSED DEPENDING ON THE ENVIRONMENT IT IS BEING USED IN.

Overhead Guard

Mast

Cab

Carriage

13

FORKLIFTS CAN EITHER BE ELECTRIC OR POWERED BY GAS. ELECTRIC FORKLIFTS ARE POWERED BY EITHER A BATTERY OR FUEL CELLS THAT PROVIDE POWER TO THE ELECTRIC MOTORS.

⚠ FUN FACT ⚠

FORKLIFT

Some heavy duty forklifts have a lifting capacity of 50 tons; that is equal to the weight of 8 elephants!

EXCAVATOR

Dipper Arm

ATTACHED TO THE END OF THE BOOM IS THE STICK OR DIPPER ARM. THE STICK PROVIDES THE DIGGING FORCE NEEDED TO PULL THE BUCKET THROUGH THE GROUND.

WHEN IT IS TIME TO START THE CONSTRUCTION PROCESS, THAT MEANS WE HAVE TO START DIGGING. EXCAVATORS ARE HEAVY PIECES OF EQUIPMENT THAT ARE GREAT FOR DIGGING LARGE DEEP HOLES WITH ITS BUCKET AND SHARP TEETH.

THEY ALSO COME IN A WIDE VARIETY OF SIZES WITH MANY DIFFERENT ATTACHMENTS. EXCAVATORS ARE ESSENTIAL ON THE JOB SITE BECAUSE THEY CAN DIG THE DEEPEST HOLES OVER ANY OTHER CONSTRUCTION MACHINE.

Glass Cab

THE GLASS OPERATOR CAB ALLOWS THE OPERATOR TO HAVE A FULL VIEW OF WHEREVER HE/SHE IS DIGGING. THERE ARE TWO LEVERS INSIDE THAT CONTROL THE BOOM AND THE BUCKET, AS WELL AS TWO PEDALS ON THE FLOOR THAT CONTROL THE DIRECTION OF THE CRAWLER TRACKS.

Bucket

ON THE END OF THE STICK IS USUALLY A BUCKET. BUCKETS HAVE NUMEROUS SHAPES AND SIZES FOR VARIOUS APPLICATIONS. THERE ARE ALSO MANY OTHER ATTACHMENTS THAT ARE AVAILABLE FOR BORING, RIPPING, CRUSHING, CUTTING, LIFTING, ETC. A WIDE, LARGE CAPACITY BUCKET WITH A STRAIGHT CUTTING EDGE IS USED FOR CLEANUP AND LEVELING, WHILE A BUCKET WITH TEETH IS USED TO BREAK THROUGH HARD GROUND AND ROCKS.

TIRES OR TRACKS?

SOME EXCAVATORS HAVE TIRES AND SOME HAVE TRACKS. THE CHOICE OF WHICH TO USE -TIRES OR TRACKS- DEPENDS ON CONDITIONS AT THE SITE AND THE JOB THAT HAS TO BE DONE.

Crawler Tracks

THE STEEL CRAWLER TRACKS HELP THE EXCAVATOR NAVIGATE THROUGH TOUGH TERRAIN SUCH AS MUD OR ICE.

Grappler

AN EXCAVATOR HAS MANY DIFFERENT ATTACHMENTS TO GET THE JOB DONE.

Augger

House

THE HOUSE ATTACHES TO THE UNDERCARRIAGE BY WAY OF A CENTER PIN, ALLOWING THE MACHINE TO SPIN 360° TO POSITION ITSELF HOWEVER IT NEEDS. THE HOUSE INCLUDES THE OPERATOR CAB, COUNTERWEIGHT, ENGINE, FUEL, AND HYDRAULIC OIL TANKS.

Dipper Arm

Boom

THE BOOM ALLOWS THE ARM OF THE EXCAVATOR TO MOVE FORWARD AND BACK AT GREAT DISTANCES TO SCOOP OR SMOOTH THE SURFACE.

Glass Cab

House

Bucket

Bucket

Under Carriage

Crawler Tracks

THE UNDERCARRIAGE INCLUDES THE BLADE, CRAWLER TRACKS, TRACK FRAME, AND A HYDRAULIC MOTOR THAT ALLOWS THE MACHINE TO DIG IN SEVERAL DIFFERENT AREAS WITHOUT HAVING TO MOVE.

⚠ FUN FACT ⚠

EXCAVATOR

The largest excavator available weighs in excess of over 2,160,510 pounds (979,990 kg); that's over 250 cars combined!

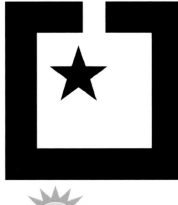

Read it. See it. Be it.

WHEEL LOADER

Hinged Joints

ALL WHEEL LOADERS HAVE HINGED JOINTS THAT ALLOW THEM THE FLEXIBILITY TO MOVE IN AND OUT OF HARD-TO-GET-TO AREAS BECAUSE IT ALLOWS THE MACHINE TO BEND IN THE MIDDLE.

Wheels

UNLIKE MOST BULLDOZERS, MOST LOADERS ARE WHEELED AND NOT TRACKED. WHEELS PROVIDE BETTER MOBILITY AND SPEED AND DO NOT DAMAGE PAVED ROADS AS MUCH AS TRACKS DO.

Tree Grabbers Forks and Claws

THERE ARE MANY DIFFERENT ATTACHMENTS FOR A WHEEL LOADER SUCH AS THE FORKLIFT THAT IS GREAT FOR MOVING PILED HIGH BOULDERS, WOOD, AND LONG PIPES.

FOR THOSE TOUGH JOBS IN THE WOODS, A HUGE BUNDLE OF TREES IS NO MATCH FOR THE WHEEL LOADER.

Bucket

THE OVERSIZED BUCKET IS CONTROLLED BY THE OPERATOR IN THE MACHINE CAB BY USING ONLY ONE JOYSTICK THAT CONTROLS ALL THE MOTIONS OF LIFT, TILT, RAISING, AND LOWERING THE BUCKET. THIS BUCKET IS VERY WIDE SO THAT IT CAN LIFT AND LOAD A LOT OF MATERIAL INTO THE BACK OF A DUMP TRUCK OR JUST MOVE MATERIALS OUT OF THE WAY.

A WHEEL LOADER HAS A FRONT-MOUNTED SQUARE, WIDE BUCKET THAT IS USED TO SCOOP UP LOOSE MATERIAL FROM THE GROUND SUCH AS DIRT, SAND OR GRAVEL, AND MOVE IT FROM ONE PLACE TO ANOTHER WITHOUT PUSHING THE MATERIAL ACROSS THE GROUND.

A LOADER IS COMMONLY USED TO MOVE A STOCKPILED MATERIAL FROM GROUND LEVEL AND DEPOSIT IT INTO AN AWAITING DUMP TRUCK OR INTO AN OPEN TRENCH EXCAVATION.

⚠ FUN FACT ⚠

WHEEL LOADER

A loader is known by many names such as bucket loader, front loader, front end loader, payloader, scoop loader, shovel, and skip loader.

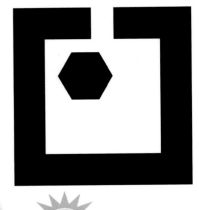

POPAR Read It. See It. Be It.

POPAR Read It. See It. Be It.

GRADER

Cab

THE CAB IS 360° TO ALLOW THE OPERATOR TO HAVE PERFECT VISIBILITY NO MATTER WHERE HE/SHE LOOKS FOR PROPERLY SMOOTHING OUT THE SURFACE.

AFTER SOME OF THE OTHER MACHINES SUCH AS THE BULLDOZER AND THE DUMP TRUCK HAVE REMOVED SOME MATERIAL SUCH AS DIRT OUT OF THE WAY, IT'S TIME TO SMOOTH EVERYTHING OUT.

Blade

THIS UNIQUE BLADE IS DRAGGED ON THE GROUND IN ORDER TO FLATTEN OUT MANY DIFFERENT SURFACES SO THEY ARE NICE AND SMOOTH FOR FURTHER WORK.

What else can graders do?

A GRADER AT WORK IN THE FARM FIELDS

GRADERS SMOOTH AND MOVE ROCKY SOIL TO MAKE ROADS

A GRADER HELPS TO CLEAR SNOW OFF THE ROADS

A GRADER, ALSO REFERRED TO AS A ROAD GRADER, A BLADE, A MAINTAINER, OR A MOTOR GRADER, IS COMMONLY USED IN THE CONSTRUCTION AND MAINTENANCE OF DIRT ROADS AND GRAVEL ROADS. IN THE CONSTRUCTION OF PAVED ROADS, THEY ARE USED TO CREATE A WIDE FLAT SURFACE FOR THE ASPHALT TO BE PLACED ON.

Cab

Blade

Weight

Grader Parts

19

⚠ FUN FACT ⚠

GRADER

In some countries, graders are also used for underground mining. In other countries, they are used to produce drainage ditches with shallow V-shaped cross-sections on either side of highways.

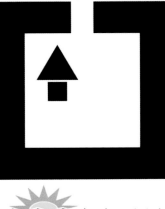

CONCRETE MIXER

CONCRETE MIXERS GENERALLY DO NOT TRAVEL FAR FROM THEIR PLANT, AS MANY CONTRACTORS REQUIRE THAT THE CONCRETE BE IN PLACE WITHIN 90 MINUTES AFTER LOADING. IF THE TRUCK BREAKS DOWN OR FOR SOME OTHER REASON THE CONCRETE HARDENS IN THE TRUCK, WORKERS NEED TO ENTER THE BARREL WITH JACKHAMMERS; DYNAMITE IS STILL USED OCCASIONALLY UNDER CERTAIN CIRCUMSTANCES, TO BREAK UP HARDENED CONCRETE IN THE BARREL.

Drum

THE DRUM IS THE LARGE MIXER THAT HOUSES THE CONCRETE UNTIL DELIVERY.

"REAR DISCHARGE" TRUCKS REQUIRE BOTH A DRIVER AND A "CHUTEMAN" TO GUIDE THE TRUCK AND CHUTE BACK AND FORTH TO PLACE CONCRETE IN THE MANNER SUITABLE TO THE CONTRACTOR.

NEWER "FRONT DISCHARGE" TRUCKS HAVE CONTROLS INSIDE THE CAB OF THE TRUCK TO ALLOW THE DRIVER TO MOVE THE CHUTE IN ALL DIRECTIONS.

Chute

WHEN THE TRUCK HAS ARRIVED AT THE LOCATION, THE CONCRETE WILL GO INTO CHUTES TO GUIDE THE VISCOUS MATERIAL DIRECTLY TO THE JOB SITE.

POURING CONCRETE FROM A "REAR DISCHARGE" TRANSPORT TRUCK

SPECIAL CONCRETE TRANSPORT TRUCKS ARE DESIGNED TO TRANSPORT AND MIX CONCRETE FROM A FACTORY/PLANT TO THE CONSTRUCTION YARD.

IF THE TRUCK CANNOT GET CLOSE ENOUGH TO THE SITE TO USE THE CHUTES, THE CONCRETE MAY BE DISCHARGED INTO A CONCRETE PUMP CONNECTED TO A FLEXIBLE HOSE, OR ONTO A CONVEYOR BELT WHICH CAN BE EXTENDED SOME DISTANCE. A PUMP PROVIDES THE MEANS TO MOVE THE MATERIAL TO PRECISE LOCATIONS, MULTI-FLOOR BUILDINGS, AND OTHER LOCATIONS.

THERE ARE TWO DIFFERENT TYPES OF TRANSPORT TRUCKS: ONE TYPE THAT IS FILLED WITH DRY MATERIALS AND WATER BECAUSE THE MIXING OCCURS DURING TRANSPORT.

THE OTHER TYPE, USED BY MORE MODERN PLANTS, LOAD THE TRUCK WITH 'READY MIXED' CONCRETE. WITH THIS PROCESS, THE MATERIAL HAS ALREADY BEEN MIXED AND THEN IS LOADED INTO THE TRUCK. THE READY-MIX TRUCK MAINTAINS THE MATERIAL'S LIQUID STATE THROUGH TURNING OF THE DRUM UNTIL DELIVERY.

Spiral Blade

THE INTERIOR OF THE DRUM ON A CONCRETE TRUCK IS FITTED WITH A SPIRAL BLADE. IN ONE ROTATIONAL DIRECTION, THE CONCRETE IS PUSHED DEEPER INTO THE DRUM. THIS IS THE DIRECTION THE DRUM IS ROTATED WHILE THE CONCRETE IS BEING TRANSPORTED TO THE BUILDING SITE. THIS IS KNOWN AS "CHARGING" THE MIXER. WHEN THE DRUM ROTATES IN THE OTHER DIRECTION, THE SPIRAL BLADE "DISCHARGES", OR FORCES THE CONCRETE OUT OF THE DRUM.

⚠ FUN FACT ⚠

CONCRETE TRANSPORT TRUCKS

Concrete transport trucks weigh 20,000 pounds (9,100 kg) to 30,000 pounds (14,000 kg), and can carry roughly 40,000 pounds (18,000 kg) of concrete.

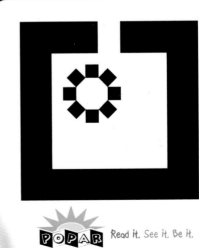

POPAR   Read it. See it. Be it.

LOADER CRANE

A LOADER CRANE (ALSO CALLED A KNUCKLEBOOM CRANE OR ARTICULATING CRANE) IS A HYDRAULICALLY-POWERED ARTICULATED ARM FITTED TO A (VEHICLE) TRAILER, AND IS USED FOR LOADING/UNLOADING THE VEHICLE.

TRADITIONALLY CONSIDERED AN UN-LOADER, KNUCKLEBOOM CRANES ARE PRIMARILY USED TO TRANSPORT MATERIALS FROM A WAREHOUSE OR YARD, TO A CUSTOMER'S YARD OR THE JOBSITE. WITH THE NEW TECHNOLOGIES OF TODAY, KNUCKLEBOOM CRANES CAN MANEUVER LIKE NO OTHER CRANE.

Boom

THE MOST RECOGNIZABLE PART OF ANY CRANE IS THE BOOM. THIS IS THE STEEL ARM OF THE CRANE THAT HOLDS THE LOAD. RISING UP FROM JUST BEHIND THE OPERATOR'S CAB, THE BOOM IS THE ESSENTIAL PIECE OF A CRANE, ALLOWING THE MACHINE TO RAISE LOADS TO HEIGHTS OF SEVERAL DOZEN FEET.

Pulley

THE PULLEY SYSTEM DELIVERS A FORCE TO MOVE THE LOAD.

Hydraulic Ram

THIS CAN BE USED DIRECTLY TO LIFT THE LOAD OR INDIRECTLY TO MOVE THE JIB OR BEAM THAT CARRIES ANOTHER LIFTING DEVICE.

Stability

PROVIDING GOOD STABILITY IS ESSENTIAL WHEN CHOOSING KNUCKLEBOOM TRUCKS. THE TRUCKS ARE NOW EQUIPPED WITH HYDRAULIC OUTRIGGERS TO PROMOTE SAFETY AND PREVENT POTENTIAL HAZARDS WHILE AT WORK.

Outriggers

Folding Capacity

THE CRANE'S CAPABILITY TO FOLD INTO A COMPACT SIZE GIVES THE ADVANTAGE OF CARRYING A LARGER PAYLOAD ON THE SAME TRUCK.

Transportability

THE CRANE IS MOUNTED ON THE KNUCKLEBOOM TRUCK WHICH ALLOWS FOR EASY TRANSPORTATION FROM ONE LOCATION TO ANOTHER.

IN THE UK AND CANADA, THIS TYPE OF CRANE IS OFTEN KNOWN AS A "HIAB", PARTLY BECAUSE THIS MANUFACTURER INVENTED THE LOADER CRANE

THE NUMEROUS JOINTED SECTIONS CAN BE FOLDED INTO A SMALL SPACE WHEN THE CRANE IS NOT IN USE.

Articulation

KNUCKLEBOOM TRUCKS CAN CONTINUOUSLY ROTATE 360° DEGREES WITH EASE. THIS FACILITATES LOADING AND UNLOADING EVEN IF THERE ARE MANY OBSTACLES IN THE WORKING AREA. THE MOUNTED CRANE CAN PIVOT FROM LEFT TO RIGHT AND VICE VERSA, THUS INCREASING PRODUCTIVITY.

WITH THE RIGHT ATTACHMENT ON A KNUCKLEBOOM CRANE, YOU CAN TURN IT INTO A SPECIALIZED PIECE OF EQUIPMENT DESIGNED TO TACKLE ABOUT ANY JOB IMAGINABLE SUCH AS TRIMMING TREES, PLACING WALLBOARD, OR PLACING CONCRETE FORMS AND THEN CLEANING UP AFTER THE JOB IS FINISHED.

23

⚠ FUN FACT ⚠

TRUCK LOADER CRANE

The first construction cranes were invented by the Ancient Greeks and were powered by men or beasts of burden such as donkeys.

Drum

SELF-PROPELLED ROLLERS MAY HAVE TWO DRUMS, MOUNTED ONE IN FRONT OF THE OTHER, UP TO THREE SIDE-BY-SIDE OR JUST ONE, WITH THE BACK ROLLERS REPLACED WITH TREADED TIRES FOR INCREASED TRACTION.

24

WATER LUBRICATION MAY ALSO BE APPLIED TO THE DRUM SURFACE TO PREVENT MATERIALS LIKE HOT ASPHALT FROM STICKING TO THE DRUM.

ON SOME MACHINES, THE DRUMS MAY BE FILLED WITH WATER ON-SITE TO ACHIEVE THE DESIRED WEIGHT. WHEN EMPTY, THE LIGHTER MACHINE IS EASIER AND CHEAPER TO TRANSPORT BETWEEN WORK SITES.

ROLLER

A ROLLER IS A COMPACTOR-TYPE ENGINEERING VEHICLE USED TO COMPACT SOIL, GRAVEL, CONCRETE, OR ASPHALT IN THE CONSTRUCTION OF ROADS AND FOUNDATIONS.

"SHEEPSFOOT" DRUM ATTACHMENTS AID THE VIBRATION COMPACTION METHOD BY ENABLING DEEPER PENETRATION OF THE MATERIALS TO BE COMPACTED.

ADDITIONAL COMPACTION MAY BE ACHIEVED BY VIBRATING THE ROLLER DRUMS, MAKING A SMALL, LIGHTWEIGHT MACHINE PERFORM AS WELL AS A MUCH HEAVIER ONE.

⚠ FUN FACT ⚠

ROLLER

In some parts of the world, road rollers are still known as steam rollers, regardless of their method of propulsion.

POPAR Read it. See it. Be it.

SAFETY

WARNING SIGNS

WITH ALL THE ROUGH GROUND AND CONSTANT MOVING, THE WORKERS NEED TO BE SECURED TO THE MACHINE SO THEY ARE SAFE FROM FALLING OUT.

ONE OF THE MOST IMPORTANT THINGS THAT A CONSTRUCTION WORKER CAN DO WHEN OPERATING ANY PIECE OF HEAVY MACHINERY IS TO WEAR HIS/HER PROTECTIVE SEATBELT.

Safety Symbols

Ear Protection Required

Hard Hats Beyond this Point

Foot Protection Required

Harness Required

THE A B C's OF HARNESS SAFETY

ANCHOR A SECURE POINT OF ATTACHMENT FOR A LIFELINE OR LANYARD.

BODY HARNESS ADJUST CHEST AND LEG STRAPS FOR PROPER FIT.

CONNECTING EQUIPMENT A LANYARD OR RETRACTABLE LANYARD CONNECTED TO A LIFELINE (ANCHOR).

UNDER CONSTRUCTION

ADDITIONAL PERSONAL PROTECTIVE EQUIPMENT IS REQUIRED WHEN DEALING WITH SITUATIONS INVOLVING HAZARDOUS SUBSTANCES WHERE WORKERS SHOULD USE PROTECTIVE GLOVES, GOGGLES, AND RESPIRATORS.

GEAR

THE TWO BIGGEST SAFETY HAZARDS ON SITE ARE FALLS FROM HIGH PLACES AND VEHICLES, BUT THERE ARE MANY MORE.

CONSTRUCTION WORKERS WEAR A HARD HAT THAT PROTECTS THEM FROM FALLING DEBRIS, ROCK, SOIL, AND MANY OTHER MATERIALS.

Hard Hat

HIGH VISIBILITY JACKETS OR BRIGHT SAFETY VESTS THAT HAVE REFLECTIVE STRIPES ARE WORN TO MAKE SURE THAT THE WORKERS CAN BE SEEN BY EQUIPMENT OPERATOR AND OTHERS, NO MATTER WHAT ENVIRONMENT THEY ARE WORKING IN.

High Visibility Vest

THESE HEAVY DUTY BOOTS ARE ESSENTIAL IN PROTECTING CONSTRUCTION WORKERS' FEET FROM EQUIPMENT, SHARP MATERIALS, ROCKS, AND LOOSE GROUND.

Steel-Toed Boots

⚠ FUN FACT ⚠

SAFETY

The construction industry is the most dangerous land-based civilian work sector. So let's play it safe and wear our safety equipment when we are ever at a job site!

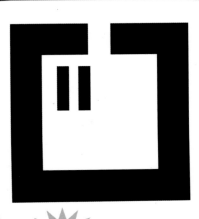

POPAR Read it. See it. Be it.

POPAR Read it. See it. Be it.

Digital Toys Here

1 Cut out Popar™ Paddles on pages 29 and 31

2 Play with Popar™ Paddles and web camera

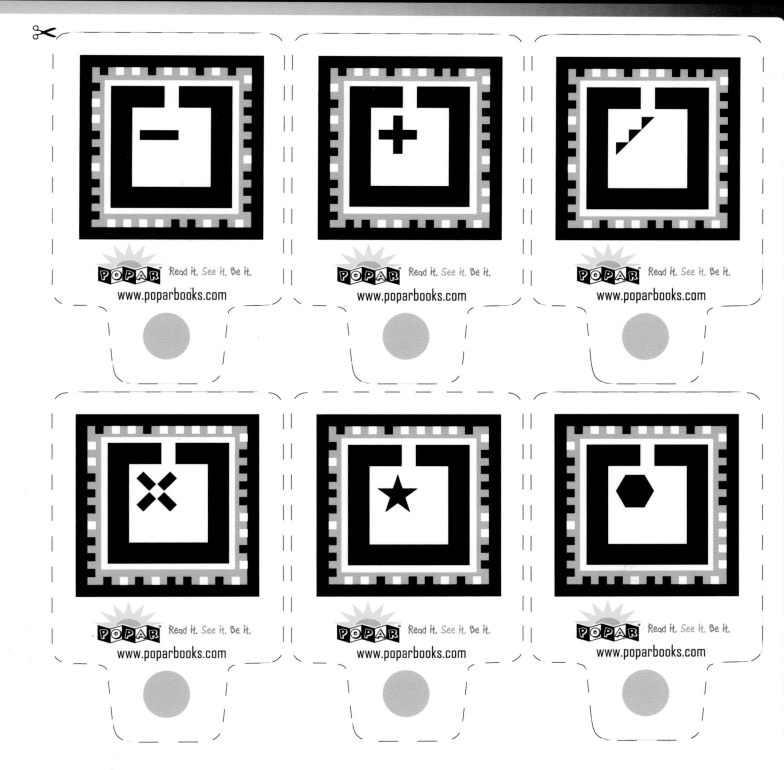

POPAR™ Read it. See it. Be it.
www.poparbooks.com

POPAR™ Read it. See it. Be it.
www.poparbooks.com

POPAR™ Read it. See it. Be it.
www.poparbooks.com

POPAR™ Read it. See it. Be it.
www.poparbooks.com

POPAR™ Read it. See it. Be it.
www.poparbooks.com

POPAR™ Read it. See it. Be it.
www.poparbooks.com

Cut out or photocopy Popar™ Paddles on this page. Use these paddles with the web camera or mobile device and software when you are not reading the book. The Popar™ Paddles have the same amazing 3D objects, just like in the story. These 3D digital toys are great to play with, take photos or capture video to share with your friends and family.

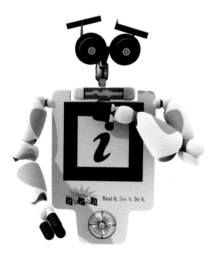

Read it. See it. Be it.
www.poparbooks.com

Read it. See it. Be it.
www.poparbooks.com

Read it. See it. Be it.
www.poparbooks.com

Read it. See it. Be it.
www.poparbooks.com

Read it. See it. Be it.
www.poparbooks.com

Read it. See it. Be it.
www.poparbooks.com

The Augmented Reality "i" Paddle that MARC-E is pointing at is what you will use throughout the entire Popar™ Books series to trigger the interaction with the 3D objects in the book or on the paddles above. These can be initiated by simply holding the "i" paddle close to any of the black and white symbols.

Get ready to...

Read it. See it. Be it.